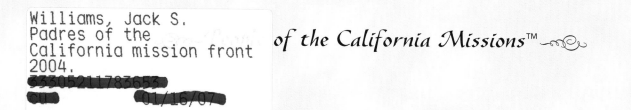

of the California Missions™

Padres
of the California
Mission Frontier

Jack S. Williams
Thomas L. Davis

The Rosen Publishing Group's
PowerKids Press™
New York

*To Francisco Palou, and the Franciscan historians who followed, and especially to
Zephyrin Engelhardt, Maynard Geiger, Francis Guest, Noel Moholy,
and Kieran McCarty, who always put the truth first, wherever it took them*

Published in 2004 by The Rosen Publishing Group, Inc.
29 East 21st Street, New York, NY 10010

First Edition

Editor: Joanne Randolph
Book Design: Corinne Jacob

Photo Credits and Illustration Credits: Cover, pp. 16, 41 courtesy of Martin J. Morgado Collection, Siempre Adelante Publishing; back cover courtesy of Jack Williams; pp. 4, 10, 14 Library of Congress Geography and Map Division; p. 4 (inset) courtesy of the Serra Cause, Old Mission Santa Barbara, photo by Thomas L. Davis; p. 6 Giraudon / Art Resource, NY; p. 9 © Craig Aurness/CORBIS; p. 10 (inset) Scala / Art Resource, NY; pp. 12, 22 courtesy of the Bancroft Library, University of California, Berkeley; pp. 17, 32, 47 courtesy of Thomas L. Davis; pp. 21, 33 drawings by Father Ignacio Tirsch, courtesy of the National Library of the Czech Republic; p. 23 courtesy of La Purisima Mission State Historic Park, California, photo © Cristina Taccone; pp. 24, 54 © Cristina Taccone ; pp. 28, 36 © North Wind Picture Archives; pp. 30, 48 Collection of Mission San Francisco de Asis, photos by Cristina Taccone; p. 31 courtesy Mission Santa Inés, photo © Cristina Taccone; pp. 38, 50 courtesy of the Karpeles Manuscript Library; p. 42 courtesy of University of Southern California, on behalf of the USC Specialized Libraries and Archival Collections; p. 44 Cindy Reiman; p. 53 Architect of the Capitol; p. 57 original art reference by Jack Williams, recreation by Corinne Jacob.

Williams, Jack S.
Padres of the California mission frontier / Jack S. Williams and Thomas L. Davis.
    p. cm. — (People of the California missions)
Summary: Describes the life and works of the Franciscan priests who helped the Spanish colonize California by establishing missions for the native peoples and new settlers.
Includes bibliographical references and index.
ISBN 0-8239-6283-0 (library binding)
1. Missions, Spanish—California—History—Juvenile literature. 2. Franciscans—California—History—Juvenile literature. 3. California—Social life and customs—18th century—Juvenile literature. 4. California—Social life and customs—19th century—Juvenile literature. 5. Indians of North America—Missions—California—Juvenile literature. 6. California—History—To 1846—Juvenile literature. [1. Missions—California. 2. Franciscans. 3. California—History—To 1846.] I. Davis, Thomas L. (Thomas Leslie), 1950– II. Title.
F864 .W735 2004
271'.30794—dc21

                              2001007871

Manufactured in the United States of America

Contents

The Franciscans and Alta California

More than two hundred years ago, a small boy named Miguel José Serra sat watching the flames of a campfire near his small home in the village of Petra. This village is on the Spanish island of Majorca, in the western part of the Mediterranean Sea. A man wearing a gray robe was telling him about strange lands and amazing people. On the other side of the Atlantic Ocean, there was another world that Europeans barely knew. They called this place the New World. The boy's life was hard. His parents were poor farmers, and the boy was often too sick to go outside and play with his friends. The stories he heard filled his head with fantastic pictures. Someday, he thought to himself, he would see that world with his own eyes.

Despite the fact that his family was very poor, this boy grew to become Junípero Serra, one of the most important individuals in the history of North America. He was the Franciscan missionary who led the first effort to colonize what is now the state of California.

Between 1769 and 1847, 142 Franciscan missionaries came to California. All of them had chosen to live according to the rules of the Roman Catholic Church and the teachings of Francis Bernardone, today known as Saint Francis.

Bernardone came from a wealthy and powerful Italian family. He was born in 1182, in Assisi, Italy. When Bernardone became an adult, he gave up his

The detail from Frederico de Wit's map of Europe, made around 1700, shows the island of Majorca off the coast of Spain. Majorca, where Junípero Serra was born, is the middle island. Junípero Serra (top inset) became a member of the Franciscan order at the age of sixteen and later left Spain to be a missionary in California.

Pope Innocent III, shown in this thirteenth-century mosaic, led the Roman Catholic Church from 1198 to 1216. He approved the founding of the religious order of men known as Franciscans.

riches in order to love and serve God. After he gave away his property, Bernardone preached to the poor and helped them. Bernardone believed strongly in the importance of and the value of nature. He even saw the animals as his spiritual brothers and sisters. Many people who also wanted to serve God were attracted to Bernardone's simple lifestyle. During Bernardone's lifetime, the leader of the Roman Catholic Church, Pope Innocent III, allowed Bernardone's followers to form a special group called a religious order. These men became known as members of the Order of Friars Minor, or Franciscans. After Bernardone died in 1226, the order continued to flourish.

The Franciscan order included religious leaders, called priests, and other men who were known as brothers. All those sent to California were priests.

This meant that they had special responsibilities to provide guidance to others and to perform ceremonies and rituals that were essential to all Roman Catholics. In California, the priests were called padres by the Spanish settlers and the Indians.

When they arrived in the region known as Alta California, or Upper California, the Franciscans discovered a land with many different topographic features. There were rocky cliffs, sandy beaches, towering mountains, immense grasslands, and hot, dry deserts. The Native American nations that lived there were also very different from one another. Each nation spoke its own language and followed its own unique customs. Some natives had religions that were similar to those of the missionaries, but most believed in gods and spirits that Europeans had never heard of or imagined. Many Indians were proud of their beliefs and were suspicious of outsiders. The padres had much to learn before any kind of a discussion about religion could begin. The Franciscans quickly realized that establishing successful missions in such a strange land would be quite difficult.

How We Know About the Padres

There are many different ways that researchers can learn about the past. Some scholars study items that were buried in the ground, such as broken bits of pottery and the ruins of buildings and even entire cities. Other specialists talk to people to see if their families remember any stories about what took place in the past. Some experts try to re-create tools that were used in the past, such as bows and arrows, to see how they worked.

We are very lucky that the Franciscans kept written records. They left behind thousands of letters, diaries, and lists that describe almost everything that they did. Other people who lived in California, including soldiers and foreign visitors, also left behind written descriptions of the padres' activities. Many of these written statements, or documents, ended up in special libraries called archives. The scholars who specialize in studying these papers are called historians. By studying the documents that people left behind, researchers are able to put together a detailed picture of the lives of many early Californians, including the padres.

Many native people died from diseases that were brought inadvertently to the California missions by European priests, traders, and explorers. Written records, such as the Book of the Dead (pictured), can help historians and researchers to understand population growth and death rates at the California missions. This particular book has Father Serra's signature in the bottom right corner.

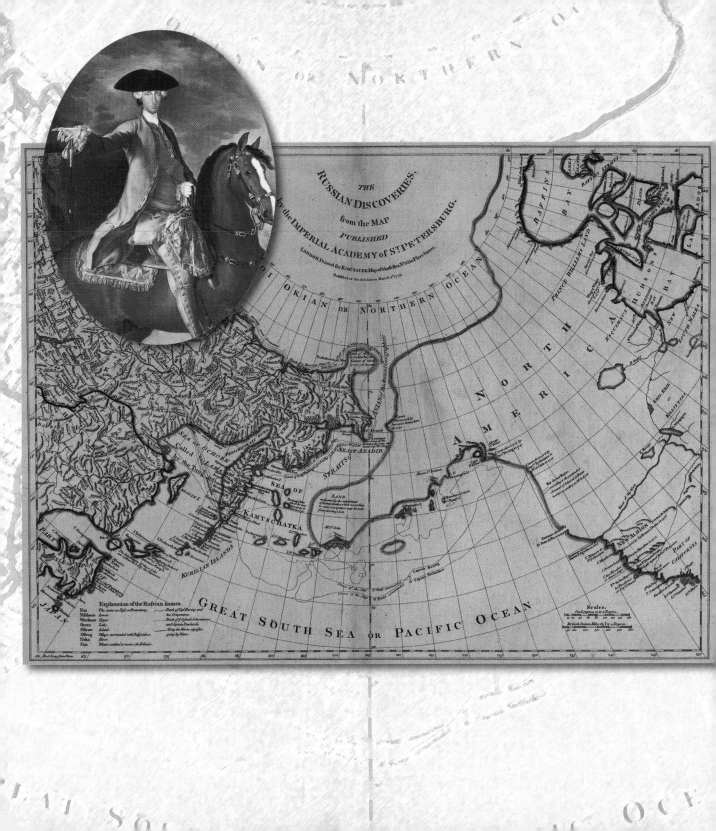

THE
RUSSIAN DISCOVERIES.
from the MAP
PUBLISHED
by the IMPERIAL ACADEMY of St. PETERSBURG.

LONDON, Printed for Robt. SAYER, Mapseller No. 53 in Fleet Street.

Published as the Act directs March 2d 1776.

OI OKIAN OR NORTHERN OCEAN

BAFFIN'S BAY

PRINCE WILLIAM'S LAND

HUDSON BAY

N O R T H

A M E R I C A

NEW SOUTH WALES

SEA OF OCHOZK

SEA OF ANADIR

STRAITS of

K A M T S C H A T K A

KURILIAN ISLANDS

NEW ALBION

PART OF CALIFORNIA

G R E A T   S O U T H   S E A   o r   P A C I F I C   O C E A N

Explanation of the Russian names.
Noss	The same as Nose or Promontory.
Nikhnee	Lower.
Werchnee	Upper.
Ozero	Lake.
Ostrow	Island.
Ostrog	Village surrounded with Palissadoes.
Reka	River.
Sim	Water neither Sea nor salt the Deluvee.

Scales.

British Statute Miles 69¼ to a Degree

Why Did the Padres Come?

The man who made the decision to colonize California was Carlos III, king of Spain. During the mid-eighteenth century, he became concerned about Russian and English exploration of the Pacific Ocean. If California was lost to another European power, its harbors could be used to launch invasions of Mexico and Peru, the two kingdoms that formed the richest parts of the Spanish Empire. In 1769, an expedition made up of sailors, soldiers, and priests was sent to conquer California. The Spanish army and navy were ordered to build military bases. The priests had another task, one that was essential to the creation of a colony in California.

Spain did not have the money, the soldiers, and the colonists needed to conquer the Native Americans who lived in California. The only way that King Carlos could save California from Russian or English claims was to build some kind of friendship with the region's Indians. Government officials decided to use missions to expand Spain's hold on the remote province. These settlements would be built as communities in which priests would teach Native Americans to live as Spaniards. The people who would be assigned to create these missions would face many challenges. They could be killed by Native Americans who might be hostile to newcomers. Before and after settlements were established, the colonists might have to deal with starvation or wild animal

Carlos III of Spain (inset) *began to worry about other countries' explorations of the Pacific Ocean and the western coast of North America. This map, published by the Imperial Academy of St. Petersburg, shows Russian exploration from that era.*

The Mission San Carlos de Carmelo padres receive their first foreign visitors, the French La Pérouse Expedition, in this sketch based on one by the expedition's artist, Gaspard Duché de Vancy. By the time of this 1786 meeting, the missionaries had converted many native Californians to Catholicism. The church on the right in the background is the one in which Father Serra was buried in 1784.

attacks. The missionaries' lives would also be threatened by storms and other natural catastrophes, such as earthquakes. Government officials selected a group of Franciscan priests to undertake this difficult and dangerous task.

Most Europeans, including Spanish officials and Franciscans, believed that the basis of civilized life was membership in the Christian religion. Therefore, they were convinced that the Californian natives had to become Christians. The government officials believed that if Native Americans adopted the Spanish beliefs and way of life, they would become loyal colonists for the king. After they joined forces with the Spanish Empire, they would be expected to defend the region against invasions by other European nations and from attacks by hostile Indians. Eventually, the Native Americans might become successful enough to send money to Spain in the form of taxes.

Becoming a Missionary

Most of the 142 Franciscans who came to California were born in Spain, which included the regions of Catalonia, Vizcaya, Valencia, Aragon, and Castille. Each region was the home of many different ethnic groups. The ancestors of the Spaniards came from Europe, Africa, and the Near East. Although the Spaniards were all Roman Catholics, each one of the ethnic and regional groups had its own customs, and several spoke their own language. The missionaries came from different parts of Spain, but almost all were raised in wealthy families.

Seventeen of the Franciscans who worked in early California came from other parts of the Spanish Empire. Twelve priests were born in Mexico, and five had spent their early life in Cuba and other parts of the Spanish Caribbean. We do not know the origins of ten of the early missionaries.

The first step on the long road that led to a job as a California missionary took place at home. In much of the Christian world, including in Spain, children spent many hours learning about their religion. As some boys grew up, they were attracted to the idea of becoming a Franciscan. Although their lives were hard, the Franciscans were loved and respected for the work that they did to help the poor. Many people were attracted to the order for the same reasons that people join religious and public service

MAPA MARITIMO
DEL GOLFO DE MEXICO
E ISLAS DE LA AMERICA,
PARA EL USO DE LOS NAVEGANTES EN ESTA
PARTE DEL MUNDO,
Construido sobre las mejores memorias, y observaciones
Astronomicas de Longitudes, y Latitudes.
Dedicado à la Catholica Magestad de
DON FERNANDO VI REY DE ESPAÑA Y DE LAS YNDIAS,
Por cuy mas Rendidos, y fieles Vasallos
Thomas Lopez, y Juan de la Cruz
Año de 1755.

MAR DEL NORTE

PENINSULA DE FLORIDA

LUISIANA

GEORGIA

GOLFO DE MEXICO

ISLAS LUCAYAS

CANAL de BAHAMA

ISLA DE CUBA

BAIA DE CAMPECHE

YUCATAN

GUAXACA

TABASCO

CHIAPA

GOLFO DE HONDURAS

ISLA
DE SANTO
DOMINGO

HONDURAS

NUEVA ESPAÑA

NICARAGUA

COSTA RICA

VERAGUA

MAR DEL SUD

DARIEN

ISLAS DE SOTTA VENTO

ISLAS ANTILLAS

Sta MARTHA

CARACAS

VENEZUELA

COMANA

AMERICA MERIDIONAL

groups today. Most sought an opportunity to understand God better. For poor people, the order offered a chance to gain an education. Some boys decided to join because of the influence of their parents. It was considered honorable to have a son or a daughter in the service of the Roman Catholic Church. The decision to become a Franciscan was extremely serious. A person who joined had to give up many things, including a great deal of personal freedom, wealth, and comfort. A boy had to be at least sixteen years old to join the Franciscans. Sometimes, parents hired tutors to prepare boys who were too young to join. Once accepted, the young recruits were sent to live in a special training center, which was called a novitiate. Here they learned just how tough it really was to be a member of the order.

Being part of a Franciscan order was a lot like being in an army. Franciscans had to follow a strict set of rules. They were not allowed to get married or to live with their families. They also had to attend many special religious ceremonies. They prayed, together and individually, many times throughout the day and night. All Franciscans had to follow the orders that they were given by their leaders without asking any questions. They could not own any property. Much of the training program stressed living without comfort or material possessions as a way of getting closer to God. Many hours were spent in other kinds of religious studies, including the analysis of historical books about the Franciscan missionaries of the twelfth and thirteenth centuries.

◄ *Working for Fernando VI, king of Spain, also called King Ferdinand, Franciscan priests Tomás Lopez and Juan de la Cruz made this maritime map of the Gulf of Mexico and its islands from memory and from astronomical observations of longitude and latitude.*

Rich decorations ornament the inside of San Fernando, the church of the Apostolic College in Mexico, shown here as it appeared around 1800. Thin sheets of gold covered the altars. The church building reflected a high level of wealth, but the Franciscans themselves dressed simply, in plain robes called habits.

The recruits were given the uniform that all Franciscans were required to wear. The most important garment was the habit. This was a robe that was held in place by a rope with three knots instead of a belt. A cross and a string of prayer beads were usually hung from the rope. The robe had a pouch that was used to store a few personal items, such as a prayer book or a diary. In California, the Franciscans' robes were gray, the color of undyed wool. In other parts of the Spanish Empire, they were blue. The Franciscans also wore sandals and sometimes wore large, flat-brimmed hats. When Franciscans became priests, they shaved the top of their head as a sign of their new life as religious leaders. When they traveled by foot, most

Padres often wore hats and used walking sticks, such as these above, as they walked from one community to another.

Franciscans carried a large wooden walking stick.

If they completed the training program, the would-be members of the order made a series of public promises, called vows. To show how important becoming a Franciscan was to them, some members of the group changed their name. For example, Junípero Serra was originally named Miguel José Serra. After the ceremony, the recruits were accepted as regular members of the order. They were ready to begin additional studies and training. When this work had been completed, they were sent to one of the many facilities that the order operated. These included hospitals, universities, schools, and missions. The Franciscans took a particular interest in helping poor people.

Most Franciscans became brothers. Some of the new members of the order decided to become priests. This required a great deal of additional study and training. It was very important that a priest understand all the ceremonies, rituals, teachings, and other skills that went into serving God and the community. Once they completed their training as priests, they often specialized in different kinds of church work, such as teaching. A few of the most talented priests became teachers at universities. Others became leaders and helped to run the many facilities operated by the order.

The long, difficult training of Franciscan priests created a sense of community within the order. However, the order did not require that its members share identical views and interests. Many Franciscans pursued activities outside of religion. For example, some priests were inventors, some studied medicine, and others became great musicians.

The Franciscan priests who became missionaries were often recruited in Spain to work in the Americas. Most wanted to serve God, and they believed that they were doing what God wanted them to do by going to California. Some were looking for a chance to share their Christian beliefs with Native Americans. Others were seeking adventure in a far-off land. A few came to California as a way of running away from their problems at home.

The priests who wanted to become missionaries had to get permission from their superiors to do so. After an individual received permission, he said good-bye to all of his relatives and friends. Very few missionaries ever got a chance to return home.

The trip to America was terrifying. The ships of the era were cramped and uncomfortable. People making the journey faced pirates, storms, and many other dangers. Once they arrived on the other side of the Atlantic, the Franciscans reported to one of a number of smaller organizations that were called apostolic colleges. These establishments worked with missions. Some colleges preached to people who were already Christians. Others focused on

Indians who had never heard of the Franciscans' faith. The College of San Fernando, in Mexico City, Mexico, was responsible for most of California's missions. The College of Our Lady of Guadalupe, in Zacatecas, Mexico, and the College of Santa Cruz, in Querétaro, Mexico, also played small parts in the development of the region's missions.

The apostolic colleges had programs that were designed to prepare the priests for their work on the frontier. There were classes on the customs and languages of the Native Americans and the methods that could be used to create and to operate missions. When a priest finally arrived in California, he reported to the head of the Franciscans who worked in the province. This man was known as the father president. The newcomer was usually assigned to work at a mission as part of a two-man team. After 1820, more and more priests had to serve alone. A few of the Franciscans spent their entire career working at one mission. Most were assigned to many different places during their time in California.

Starting a New Mission

Government officials, and not Franciscans, had the right to order that a new mission be established. They provided the priests with the name for the mission and selected the general area for the new settlement. An expedition made up of Franciscans, soldiers, and Christian Indians usually was sent to find a home for the new community. These men searched for a place with a large population of native people and a good supply of water and farmland. The first father president, Junípero Serra, required that the priests visit the leaders of the local Native American village and receive an invitation to stay in the area before any mission site could be considered. Once everyone had agreed, there was a ceremony, and the expedition set up a large wooden cross.

In the early days, the missions were very simple. A settlement's buildings usually included a few huts and a crude wooden church. Typically, a long time passed before any native people came to live at the mission. The priests and soldiers often feared Native American attacks. They sometimes built log walls to protect their tiny communities.

Most of the early missionaries were shocked when they first saw Native Americans. The people of California's first nations were very different from Europeans and even Mexican Indians. They did not wear much clothing.

In this painting by Padre Ignacio Tirsch, Mission San José del Cabo, in the foothills of San Lucas, Baja California, is depicted with a Philippine galleon arriving to be supplied with food. Events such as this one also regularly took place in Alta California. ➤

These California Indians, who are decorated with paint and feathers, were drawn at Mission San José de Guadalupe by German artist Wilhelm von Tilenau during a Russian exploring expedition in 1806.

They ate things that were not part of the European diet, such as snakes and insects. Their views about marriage were very different from those of the Europeans. The native languages were hard for Europeans to understand.

The way the padres worked through their initial feelings was very important to their overall relationship with the native people. Some priests were never able to see through the differences and accept the Native Americans as fellow human beings. However, most Franciscans quickly grew to admire many of the Indians' customs. They shared the Indians' love of nature and the importance they placed on community. They also respected the Native Americans' customs involving cleanliness and were touched by the parents' love for their children.

As soon as the cross was set up, the missionary team began negotiations designed to persuade people to move into their settlement. The priests began their work with offers of gifts. These items usually consisted of food, jewelry, and pieces of cloth. Once they had visited with the Franciscans, the Native Americans saw the opportunity to get a number of other practical objects, such as axes, knives, needles, and clothing. The Franciscans

Many Native Americans enjoyed listening to European-style music, which was taught at the missions' schools. This songbook for a choir was used at Mission La Purísima.

also had many beautiful things, including paintings, statues, religious rituals, and music. The soldiers who accompanied the priests brought powerful weapons, such as firearms and steel swords. The priests and the soldiers would make powerful allies if the Indians went to war with enemy nations.

Some of the Native Americans were attracted to the missions because of the Franciscans' preaching. Many of the priests talked of the chance to build a perfect world, or a utopia. As does the world today, the Native American world had many problems. Some people were treated unfairly. Others did not like, or did not believe, the religious ideas that they heard from their leaders.

The priests called the Indians who decided to become Christians neophytes, or new followers. Once the Native Americans had moved into the settlements, the Franciscans made sure that the Native Americans understood that they were not slaves. The neophytes were allowed to visit and trade with non-Christian people, whom the Spaniards called gentiles. The Indians at the missions sometimes persuaded their relatives to come to live with them. The Franciscans explained to the Indians that, although the priests were in charge of the outposts, they did not own them. All the possessions that the missions contained, all the animals, the fields, and the lands, belonged to the neophytes. In time, the Franciscan priests would leave the settlements to begin new missions. Then the Native Americans would be put in charge of the settlements.

This bell wall at the San Diego mission has been restored to the way it looked when it rang to signal prayer, work, or mealtime in the California mission days.

In the meantime, the neophytes were expected to trust the priests as their overall leaders. Life in the early missions had many rules. There was plenty of hard work to do, even though the neophytes had more vacation days than we do today. The mission bells often rang to let the whole community, including the missionaries, know that it was time for another activity. Most neophytes were expected to work about six hours each day. Their assignments did not always make them happy.

Sometimes people refused to work or even ran away. Other Native Americans broke the rules against stealing and fighting.

The priests had to find some way to keep order. The most obvious way to enforce the rules was to use the soldiers who served as mission guards. However, if the padres depended on the mission guards too much, there was a danger that the native community as a whole would rebel or simply run away. The neophytes had weapons, and they usually outnumbered the Franciscans and soldiers by more than ten to one. In contrast with central Mexico, Spain had no large armies in California that could help to control the neophytes.

To remain in control, the missionaries had to cooperate with the neophytes and find common goals. Before the Europeans arrived, the Native Americans had looked to their village leaders to keep order, so the missionaries worked closely with native leaders. The Franciscans usually concentrated their diplomatic skills on these men. At many missions, the priests' efforts seem to have succeeded. Many village chiefs brought their communities to live with Franciscans at the new settlements.

Once the village leaders had been won over, they could act as a mission council to represent the groups within the Indian community. The padres had to balance carefully their rules with the needs of the Spanish government and the desires of their native followers. By working through traditional leaders, the priests could get the neophytes to enforce the rules themselves.

Not all Franciscans were skilled in creating relationships with Native American officials. The best of the diplomats was probably Antonio Peyri of

Mission San Luis Rey. He was able to accomplish an amazing amount in a very short period of time. Other Franciscans were not so successful. At a few of the missions, large groups of Indians simply walked away from their new homes. At other outposts, there was constant fear and suspicion among both the neophytes and the newcomers.

Many other circumstances affected the success and the progress of the early missions. A great deal depended on the attitudes of the native people. When friendship was forged with the newcomers, the missions quickly grew. Another important factor was the language differences of the people living together in the missions. When all the Native Americans could understand one basic language, as at Mission Santa Barbara, things went well. By contrast, at Mission Santa Clara, different groups of neophytes who lived there at the same time spoke as many as twenty different languages. This made communication almost impossible and slowed the mission's progress. There were many other possible problems that could slow progress. In some places, floods, epidemics, earthquakes, and attacks by other Indians almost eliminated the communities.

Of the twenty-three missions that were established in California, only the two settlements founded in 1781 on the Colorado River were abandoned. Native Americans who were against the missions destroyed both of these outposts less than one year after they were established. The rest of the California missions survived to become permanent communities.

Running the Missions

Once a mission had been established and had attracted a population of Native Americans, the Franciscans could supervise their Indian community in a more direct way. One of the padres usually worked full-time to meet the neophytes' religious needs. A second priest concentrated his efforts on the other activities that took place at the mission, such as farming and ranching.

Both padres worked closely with native leaders. Village chiefs and other cooperating elders were formed into a kind of town government. The neophyte leaders made up the main police force of the missions. The troops who guarded the settlements became involved only when a serious crime, such as a murder, was committed.

The padres also appointed many other leaders. The head of the soldiers who formed the guard was in charge of the mission's defense. Translators helped with religious instruction. Dozens of Native American bosses carried out the orders of the padres and the town council. Everyone had a job and knew whom to go to for instructions.

The Padres and the Religious Life of the Missions

The priests struggled to teach religion to the neophytes. The Indian people were quick to copy and learn the outward signs of their new faith. They also

understood that the priests did not want them to continue their old beliefs and religious customs. Some made the changes that the Franciscans wanted. Many more continued to practice their old beliefs along with Christianity. However, some priests felt that the neophytes were more committed to living as good Christians than were the soldiers and the settlers of nearby towns and presidios.

The missionary who was in charge of the religious life of the community was a very busy man. Besides running the services, he had to plan many other ceremonies. Some of these celebrations were determined by the calendar. There were hundreds of feast days and special rituals.

The missionaries provided services for the neophytes. They also held celebrations for holy days. There were different rituals for babies, older children, and adults. The priests visited sick people and gave them special prayers. The padres also attended to their followers' funerals and burials.

There were dozens of religious records and catalogs to be prepared. The padres recorded carefully all the ceremonies provided to individual neophytes. With feather pens and ink, they listed people's names, ages, places of birth, and other essential information. Some of these records had to be summarized for the Spanish government, as well as for the father president.

Many hours were spent inside the mission church. This was the largest and most decorated building in each community. The frontier churches looked different from modern ones. There were only a few benches. During the religious ceremonies that were held inside, nearly everyone stood up or knelt. During services, a special material called incense was burned in small

Priests and neophytes of the Pala Mission congregate at a mass for
◄ *the dead in this 1883 hand-colored engraving by Henry Sandham.*
The engraving first appeared in Century Magazine *in 1883.*

 29

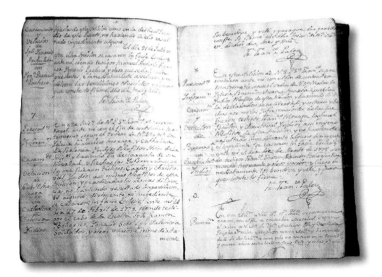

This marriage register from the Mission San Francisco de Asís documents the first marriage of an Ohlone Indian couple overseen by the missionaries in 1776.

metal containers. The smoke filled the church with wonderful smells. Dozens of colorful paintings and statues of saints lined the walls. Many of the decorations were made using Native American symbols.

At one end of the hall was a low platform that was separated from the rest of the space inside the church by a short, wooden railing. Set against the wall was a large, tablelike structure, called the main altar. On top of the altar, there was a set of sacred objects, including a book of prayers, which priests used during important ceremonies. On one side of this sacred space, a stairway led to a small tower, called a pulpit. From there the priests made announcements, read the Bible aloud, and gave speeches.

Near the main entrance of the church was a larger, wooden platform with a railing, called a choir loft, which the native singers and musicians reached by using a set of stairs. The music that was played during religious services was sometimes serious, but more often was filled with joy.

On one side of the altar, a doorway led to a separate, small room. Here, other religious equipment, including special clothing, was stored. This room was called the sacristy. The padres used many different types of garments for ceremonies. They also had dozens of religious items that were used for various rituals.

The ceremonies that were held in the churches were designed to have an important impact on the neophytes' lives. When the priests brought their followers together here, the priests wanted them to feel at home and to feel as if they were a part of a larger family that extended to all Christians.

These vestments were worn by padres at the Mission Santa Inés.

Some religious festivals were celebrated outside the church. These events were often the most exciting days of the year. All work at the mission would stop. Every member of the community took part. Many of the holidays involved combinations of sacred parades, solemn songs, and many hours of prayers. However, it would be a mistake to think that all these events were serious. Some religious events were filled with wild celebrations that could last for several days. The missionaries encouraged the neophytes to make fun of the devil with songs, dances, and plays. Many holidays included fireworks displays.

A chalice is a sacred object that is used by priests during Holy Communion.

It took a lot of extra work and time to organize the major holidays. The people had to make decorations, prepare special meals, gather flowers, and clean the mission. The priests had to organize the neophytes and set aside the time needed to complete each task.

The efforts to take care of the church and all the religious equipment never ended. There were special rules involved in most tasks. This was a big job, and there were rarely any people around, except for the missionaries, who understood all the right ways of handling sacred objects and equipment.

The Franciscans' congregations, or groups of followers, were often large. One priest might be responsible for more than one thousand Indians, as well as the colonists living in nearby towns and military bases. Not everyone could come to the mission to hear the padres preach. As a result, the Franciscans sometimes had to travel to all those communities to visit their congregations. This meant that they had to spend many days away from home each month. The padres were often seen riding horses, mules, and donkeys. Some of the priests preferred to walk, in imitation of Christ and Saint Francis. The missionaries would crisscross the mission territory as they went from one religious ceremony to the next. It was not unusual for a padre to have to hold major ceremonies in four or five different places on a single Sunday.

The Padres as Teachers

Usually one of the two priests who worked at the mission focused his efforts on running the other areas of the community's activities. To be considered a responsible member of Spanish society, neophytes were expected to learn European ways of doing things. They also needed to wear Spanish-style clothing and learn how to use European tools. The church was the heart of the religious activities, and each of the settlements was also a kind of school. The padres taught Spanish, music, and dozens of practical skills, such as farming, ranching, and woodworking. Whenever possible, the

This painting by Ignacio Tirsch shows a farm located 3 miles (5 km) away from San José del Cabo, in Baja California. The padres taught the neophytes how to raise animals and farm the land.

missionaries hired European colonists and mission guards from the military bases to help them.

At first all the training took place out-of-doors. There were usually many problems with communication. Over time, the padres learned the Native Americans' languages, and almost every neophyte was taught Spanish. However, some neophytes learned the language more quickly than did others. The best students became translators for the padres. Those who wanted to learn more were taught to read and write.

Almost all the Native Americans showed an immediate interest in the padres' music. From the Franciscans' hand signals and other simplified symbols, the neophytes were able to learn even the most complicated kinds of church music. The larger missions had native choirs and small orchestras. Foreign visitors praised the neophytes' talents as singers and musicians.

For some of the jobs at the mission, such as woodworking and farming, instruction took place where the tasks were performed. For these and similar trades, the teaching was usually done by example.

The Franciscans were not experts at the kinds of work performed by women. They usually hired a soldier's wife or a native woman who had already learned the techniques used in European-style homes to teach and supervise the older neophyte girls. In general, the Franciscans did not try to eliminate completely the traditional native customs. Most Native Americans were happy to add new ideas to their old, familiar ones.

The Padres as Builders

The Franciscans believed that the neophytes deserved to live in comfortable, modern settlements. The early log-and-thatch structures were quickly replaced by those made from earthen blocks, called adobes. Most early adobe buildings were little more than mud boxes. However, after 1790, the missionaries began to create more sophisticated buildings. The foreign visitors who came to California were amazed by the magnificent constructions. The Franciscans and their hired architects supervised the neophytes as they assembled massive churches, aqueducts, dams, fountains, hospitals, mills, orchards, warehouses, and factories. At many of the missions, the neophytes had houses that were as comfortable as those of the colonists who lived in towns and military bases.

The Padres' Work on the Farms and Ranches

The job of running the community's farms and ranches often challenged the padres. The older missions owned thousands of cattle, horses, and sheep, and they grew enough crops to support a much larger population than the missions actually had. The day-to-day operation of the mission ranches and farms employed hundreds, even thousands, of workers. Dozens of different tasks had to be organized and completed on schedule. Everyone who lived in the settlements shared in the work, the products, and the harvests.

There was always a new set of tasks to be done. The calendar was filled with work such as planting, weeding, harvesting, and gathering livestock. Nearly all the crops and meat that the missions' fields and herds produced had to be stored in warehouses. Eventually the food was distributed to the people. The padres wanted to make sure everyone got his or her fair share, so all the goods were carefully counted and recorded before being given away.

At the larger missions, the padres eventually established ranches and farms away from the main settlement. Once these outposts had been created, the priests had to visit them from time to time to ensure their success.

Some items that the missions used, such as chocolate, made from cacao, could not be produced in California. These goods were imported from other regions.

The Padres' Work in the Development of Industries and Trade

The Franciscans wanted to provide the neophytes with more than simple food and shelter. They also wanted the Native Americans to have European-style wooden furniture, clothing, pottery, and similar luxury goods.

To create some of these items, the padres built factories at some of the missions. Craftsmen hired by the Spanish government helped to train the neophytes. Many different kinds of products were made, including furniture, cloth, blankets, ironwork, saddles, soap, pottery, and shoes.

The Franciscans would have preferred that each mission produce everything that it needed or wanted. However, items such as glass beads and food such as chocolate, from tropical regions, could not be easily produced in California. At first, there was little money available to purchase such things. However, after 1790, additional money was made available by the sale of cattle hides to foreign merchants. Most of the new cash was spent to improve the mission buildings and to buy luxury goods for the Native Americans. Soon some of the neophytes at the most prosperous missions had more of these items than the colonists at the towns and military bases. The padres had to keep careful records of the missions' industrial activities. They were often asked to provide reports for government and church officials back in Spain and Mexico.

The Padres and Health at the Missions

The Franciscans wanted the neophytes to live healthy lives. They were troubled because European diseases killed many of the native peoples in a way that the padres could not understand. The padres did not realize that Spaniards rarely became seriously ill from these sicknesses because their ancestors had been exposed to the diseases for hundreds of years. Over time, the people who had a natural resistance to a disease lived longer and had more children than those who did not. Eventually, Europeans as a whole became more resistant to these diseases. The Native Americans did not have this resistance.

The padres often worked as doctors, because they were the most educated men in California. To improve the neophytes' health, they brought European medicines and healing techniques to the missions. Unfortunately, medical

The president of the California missions, Father Estevan Tapis, acknowledges the receipt of instructions for performing cesarean section operations in the year 1804, from his office at the Santa Bárbara mission.

knowledge during mission times was very primitive. Many so-called cures were worse than the diseases. One common treatment for almost every kind of sickness was to cut the wrist of a sick person to let the "bad" blood out. The priests often experimented with native cures that used herbs and plants. When it became obvious that a community was suffering from diseases, the Franciscans built hospitals with rows of beds and separate sections for men and women. Despite the priests' healing efforts, more Native Americans died than were born each year at the missions.

The Padres' Other Activities

The Franciscan missionaries provided religious leadership for the soldiers and settlers of early California. The government required them to serve at the military bases and towns. There were no other priests available in the province.

The missionaries also found work as government explorers. They often left their communities for several weeks to make journeys into the unknown parts of the interior of California. The information that they collected was used by the army and the missionaries to plan new missions.

Many of the Franciscans were interested in working in other areas part-time. Some padres spent their spare hours recording native languages and customs. A few members of the order spent their time writing histories of what happened and descriptions of the new plants and animals that they came across.

The Daily Schedule

The padres had busy lives. On workdays, they got up before dawn. They started their morning with prayers and took time to think about God. At 7:00 A.M. the padres led the first service and religious class for the Native Americans. They and their followers then ate breakfast. At about 9:00 A.M. the bell rang, and everyone went about his or her other work.

The first break of the day took place at about 11:00 A.M. The church bell rang, and the entire community stopped for the main meal of the day. At noon, the padres returned to the church for their midday prayers. Most of the padres took advantage of the next few hours to rest. When the bell sounded again, people returned to their jobs. There was a short break at 3:00 P.M. for additional prayers.

At dusk, the community stopped their activities and gathered in the church for more prayers and lessons. This was followed by the evening meal and a short period of relaxation. Finally at about 9:00 P.M. the padres went into their rooms for sleep and private prayers. With all the work they had to do, the Franciscans rarely had a moment of spare time.

For most of the people living in the missions, Sundays and holidays provided a break in the regular schedule. However, for the missionaries these days involved even more hard work.

Father Serra died in this celdilla, or cell, at Mission Carmel on August 28, 1784. Historians rebuilt the room in 1937. The only items that actually belonged to Serra are the disciplina on the wall, and possibly the Bible (not shown). Inset: The San Juan de la Crus bell, from 1781, is the oldest remaining bell at Mission Carmel.

Life at Home

When they were not working, the Franciscans usually could be found in their mission homes. These buildings were called *conventos* in Spanish, and friaries in English. These structures were usually built in the main square that stood next to the church. The adobe conventos often had many rooms and looked large from the outside. However, the Franciscans actually slept individually in tiny rooms. Simple beds, writing desks, and prayer stools were the rooms' only furniture. Most of the time, the priests had one blanket each, even when it was very cold. A cross or a religious painting sometimes hung on the wall. The padres often spent more time praying than they did sleeping in their bedrooms. Every member of the order was supposed to pray at least seven times each day. The padres usually slept from three to four hours each night. All the Franciscans, even the father president, had sleeping areas that were much less comfortable than those of the soldiers or neophytes.

The conventos at the most successful missions also included some other rooms that were more inviting. There was usually a main living room equipped with comfortable chairs and couches. Though women were not allowed in the convento, this area was used for recreation and to entertain male guests. A similar room equipped with a massive table served as a dining hall. Most conventos also had a library that served as an office. Here the priests sat with

The Franciscans lived in buildings called conventos. The conventos usually stood next to the church. The padres had their own small rooms within the larger building. This image shows what the great stone church at San Juan Capistrano may have looked like before an earthquake destroyed it.

pen and ink and recorded the lives of the people in their congregations, late into the evenings. The walls of these parts of the convento were decorated with religious paintings and designs that were similar to those used in the churches. The floors were often covered with tiles. The rooms were heated with large, open, metal baskets filled with hot coals.

The padres' meals were usually prepared in a large adobe kitchen built either next to or near the convento. This building was equipped with stoves and ovens. The foods that were eaten were similar to today's Mexican dishes. Many recipes were prepared using tortillas, bread, milk, eggs, vegetables, and fresh fruit. On special occasions, the padres ate more elaborate meals made with fish, cheese, sausages, ham, and beef.

The Franciscans who worked in the larger missions were so busy that they had to depend on neophytes to help keep up their quarters. The native people usually cooked, did the laundry, and swept and scrubbed the floors.

Although they spent a lot of time at work, the Franciscans enjoyed

Although they were sworn to serve God, the Franciscans enjoyed many pastimes, including playing cards.

some pleasurable aspects of life. The padres drank large amounts of hot chocolate. When they got together with other Franciscans, they sometimes played cards, checkers, or chess. Not everything that they studied involved religion. They spent many hours reading magazines and newspapers from Mexico and Spain. They also read books on science, engineering, and history, and they even read novels. Some of the Franciscans were excellent hunters. As did most practical frontier people, they knew as much about guns as did the soldiers.

Retirement

The Franciscans who arrived before 1821 were expected to serve for at least ten years as part of the arrangement that was worked out by the king and the Franciscan officials. They averaged about sixteen years in California. Life in the missions was hard and illness was common. Padre José Ramón Abella held the record for length of service. He managed to work for forty-four years. Although the padres often traveled in dangerous places, only six of the Franciscans who worked in California died at the hands of Native Americans. Four of these people were killed in 1871, in the missions built on the Colorado River. One died in San Diego in 1775, and one other individual was killed at Mission Santa Cruz in 1812. One of the reasons that the missionaries were able to survive was through the kindness and protection provided by the friendly Native Americans. In general, the neophytes did an excellent job of protecting the padres and the missions.

When a missionary could no longer work, he had several options. Many of the Franciscans decided to stay in California and serve the Indians as best they could until they died. Of the 127 men from the College of San Fernando who came, a total of 58 were buried in the province. The rest were allowed to return to Mexico City, to live in the apostolic college. A few retired to Spain.

These Franciscans lived in Mission Santa Bárbara in the nineteenth century. They are the last surviving Spanish and Mexican Franciscans who worked at the California missions. This photograph was taken around 1860.

Unfinished Missions

Between 1769 and 1835, the padres created and ran twenty-three California missions. Some of the missions were more successful than others. All but two of these communities grew into important settlements. In a few places, the padres and the Native Americans seemed to have become close friends. However, in the end, none of the neophytes were given control of their lands, or of the wealth that they had helped to create.

From the start, the Spanish government officials had seen the missions as a way to get what they wanted by using Indians. The Franciscans, who did not control the government, came for other reasons. They wanted to see the Indians become Christians and live in peace as part of the Spanish Empire. They knew that some people in the government did not have any intention of helping the Indians. However, in the end, they felt that the king would make sure that the neophytes were protected and treated well.

When army officials arrived in California, they thought it was fine that the missionaries had made peace with the Indians. However, as the European settlers grew stronger, many soldiers believed that the military governor should be placed in charge of working with the Native Americans.

Between 1770 and 1781, the Franciscans' enemies tried to get the king to eliminate or limit the padres' work in California. They reminded the king that

This painting is of Saint Francis, founder of the Franciscans,
◄ *witnessing an Ohlone Indian wedding. The Franciscan and Indian ways of life are shown coming together.*

Narcisco Duran, who served as president of the missions for many years, argued against the dissolution of the mission system in this historical document.

other missions, such as those built in Florida, had failed. The army officials wanted to make friends with the Indians through trade and to let the native peoples continue their old ways of doing things. In time, the enemies of the Franciscans said that they would bring enough colonists from Spain and Mexico to replace the Native Americans. There was no real need to teach the Native Americans about God, or about anything else. The existence of the mission towns would only make it harder for the European settlers to get their hands on land and other resources.

The differences between the army officials and the Franciscans led to bitter fights. In the end, the king decided to leave the Franciscans in control of the missions. As long as a Spanish king ruled California, there were no more serious challenges to the idea that the padres should run the missions.

In 1821, California became a part of the new nation of Mexico. In the capital, Mexico City, officials fought a long battle over the part played by the Catholic Church in government programs. By 1824, the group that opposed the church had won. The word went out that the California missions would be shut down. The neophytes would become citizens, and they would receive their lands and other properties.

When the Franciscans heard about what was going to happen, they became very upset. The padres believed that some of the missions had Indians who might be ready for these changes, but that in most places the Indians still had much to learn. The Franciscans were also afraid that some of the settlers would steal the Native Americans' lands and other property. Throughout the colonial world, Indian nations had lost everything to European settlers. The surviving Native Americans were often made slaves or were forced to live on the worst lands. The padres knew all about what had happened in most of the Americas, and they were determined not to let similar events take place in California.

Between 1824 and 1833, the padres managed to convince government officials to block the elimination of the missions. However, the elected leaders in Mexico City and the many settlers who lived in California wanted to end the Franciscans' work as Indian agents. There were also many Native Americans who believed that, under the new system, they would have more freedom and control over their own lives. Without knowing or understanding what might happen, they trusted the Mexican government to protect them as citizens.

Between 1833 and 1835, the Franciscan missions were officially brought to an end. In the five years that followed, the padres' worst fears came to pass. The neophytes lost everything. Greedy settlers grew rich off the Indians' hard work. Conflicts between the Mexicans and the Indian nations in California grew worse. Many of the native people became slaves at the farms and ranches of the wealthy landowners. Others wandered the highways in search of food, without either homes or hope. The mission churches and most of their surrounding settlements fell into ruins. If you looked hard, you could find a handful of padres serving the Native Americans who still came there in search of help. Stripped of all their powers as agents for the neophytes, the Franciscans could do almost nothing to help the Native Americans.

The Franciscan Heritage

Today evidence of the work of the early Franciscans can be seen throughout California. The missions that they ran still survive as museums and churches.

Most of the names that they placed on the land, such as San Luis Obispo, San Francisco, and Santa Bárbara, have remained. Famous cities and towns grew from the missions that the padres and the Indians built. In almost every city and town that they lived in or near, streets are named for important Franciscans. The way missions look, with their red roof tiles, bell towers, and massive white walls, has been copied into almost every kind of building that you can name, from supermarkets to train stations. In the Statuary Hall in the U.S. Capitol in Washington, D.C., each state is represented by two figures that symbolize the best qualities of that American state. One of the statues that represent California is Junípero Serra.

Although most historians and modern residents have honored the Franciscans, not everyone thinks that the missions were a good way to colonize California.

In 1930, Ettore Cadorin of Venice, Italy, made a bronze sculpture of Father Junípero Serra. It can be seen at the Capitol's Statuary Hall in Washington, D.C.

They believe that it was bad for the Franciscans to try to teach the Indians their religion and how to live as Spaniards. It is also true that many Indians died at the missions from European diseases, and from other events that happened as a result of the arrival of newcomers to California, such as warfare. In the end, the neophytes were not given control of their lands and the other property that they had helped to create. To some people who dislike all the parts of the colonial system, the missions were nothing but failed promises and graves.

It is easy to find faults in the actions of some of the early Franciscans and in the history of the missions. It is clear that the padres did not create the kind of heaven on earth that they had hoped for and had strived to achieve. Some of the missionaries behaved badly and hurt Indians, or failed to live by the high standards that the padres set for other people. Even the best padres made mistakes that resulted in native suffering, and sometimes in death.

However, the story of the Franciscans in early California can be seen in a more positive light. In a time when most Europeans said that Native Americans were not human beings, the missionaries saw them as their brothers, sisters, and children. Most government officials accepted that Indians should be killed or driven away, but the padres tried to find a place for them in their world. Although most Europeans saw the Native Americans as inferior in every way, some of the Franciscans found the Native Americans to be beautiful and wise. When government officials tried to take the native peoples' lands and property, the padres fought them until the padres were no longer in a position to provide any help.

◄ *This photo shows the Mission San Luis Rey facade and convento as it exists today.*  55

Amid the confusion and the dramatic changes brought about by the Europeans who settled in California, the missionaries offered the Native Americans a vision of hope. Native Americans and Franciscans joined to try to build their Californian utopia. The plan failed for many reasons, but for a brief period of time, in a few places, the missions connected the European and Native American worlds in friendship. The padres and the Indians worked together and lived prosperous, productive lives. Outside changes brought the world of the California missions to an early end, leaving behind magnificent buildings and stories of a time when Native Americans and Franciscans tried to build a better future in peace for both of their peoples.

Even today, a person can find Franciscans living in the California missions. At San Luis Rey, San Antonio, San Miguel, and their headquarters at Santa Bárbara, Franciscans can be seen living much as they have since 1769. If someone is lucky enough to spend some time with them, he or she might see the spark of energy and faith that made the early Franciscans travel to California not to govern or to become rich, but to help the Indians and to share something they felt was precious.

✝ San Francisco Solano

✝ San Rafael Arcángel

Presidio
de San
Francisco ◆

✝ San José

✝ Santa Clara de Asís
● Pueblo de San José

Santa Cruz ✝ Pueblo de Branciforte
✝ San Juan Bautista

Presidio de
San Carlos
de Monterey ◆ ✝ San Carlos Borromeo
de Carmelo

✝ Nuestra Señora de la Soledad

✝ San Antonio de Padua

✝ San Miguel Arcángel

✝ San Luis Obispo de Tolosa

✝ La Purísima Concepción

✝ Santa Inés

✝ Santa Bárbara

Presidio de Santa Bárbara ◆

✝ San Buenaventura

San Fernando
✝ Rey de España

Pueblo de ●
Los Angeles ✝ San Gabriel
Arcángel

✝ San Juan
Capistrano

✝ San Luis Rey
de Francia

Presidio de San Diego ◆ ✝ San Diego
de Alcalá

Glossary

adobes (uh-DOH-beez) Earthen blocks that are made with mud and straw or grass.

apostolic colleges (a-puh-STAH-lik KAH-lij-ez) Organizations of missionaries who specialized in preaching.

aqueducts (A-kweh-dukts) Channels used to carry water.

archives (AR-kyvz) Special kinds of libraries where documents that have not been published and similar materials are stored.

choir loft (KWY-er LOFT) A wooden platform on which people and musicians sing and perform during certain kinds of religious services.

congregations (kahn-gruh-GAY-shunz) Groups of people who come together to the same house of worship.

conventos (kuhn-VEN-tohs) A Spanish word for places where members of a religious order live.

documents (DOK-yoo-ments) Any kind of written records.

expedition (ek-spuh-DIH-shun) A group of people who have come together to undertake a military operation or exploration.

Franciscans (fran-SIS-kinz) Members of a religious group founded by Saint Francis of Assisi, an important medieval reformer of the Roman Catholic Church.

friaries (FRYR-eez) Places where friars live. Friars are members of religious orders who move from place to place. Other orders include monks, who usually spend their lives in one place, normally called a monastery.

gentiles (JEN-tylz) A word used by missionaries for Native Americans who were not Christians.

habit (HA-bit) The uniform worn by the Franciscans.

industrial activities (in-DUS-tree-ul ak-TIH-vih-teez) Actions that take place in connection with the large-scale production of goods.

mills (MILZ) Devices used to grind grains into powder.

neophytes (NEE-uh-fyts) Native Americans who became Christians.

novitiate (noh-VIH-shee-uht) A Franciscan training center.

padres (PAH-drayz) A term, borrowed from Spanish, that means "fathers."

presidios (preh-SEE-dee-ohs) Military colonies in northern New Spain. In California, all the presidios were protected by fortifications.

religious order (ree-LIH-jus OR-dur) A religious organization within the Catholic Church that has its own set of rules and customs. The Franciscans were known as the Order of Friars Minor.

sacristy (SA-kruh-stee) A room where religious equipment and sacred clothing are stored.

superiors (soo-PEER-ee-urz) People, especially heads of a religious order, who are above other people in rank.

topographic (tah-puh-GRA-fik) Of or relating to the shapes and forms of the land in a particular region.

utopia (yoo-TOH-pee-uh) A kind of ideal community in which everyone is treated fairly and is happy.

vows (VOWZ) Sacred promises.

Resources

There are many places that you can learn more about early California and daily life in the pueblos and ranches. The following lists provide information about some of the more important resources.

Books:

DeNevi, Don, and Noel Francis Moholy. *Junípero Serra: The Illustrated Story of the Franciscan Founder of California's Missions.* San Francisco: HarperCollins, 1985.

Webb, Edith. *Indian Life at the Old Missions.* Lincoln, Nebraska: University of Nebraska Press, 1983.

Museum:

Mission San Carlos Borromeo. 3080 Rio Road, Carmel, California 93923. (831) 624-3600. (www.carmelmission.org)

Web Sites:

Due to the changing nature of Internet links, PowerKids Press has developed an online list of Web sites related to the subject of this book. This site is updated regularly. Please use this link to access the list:

www.powerkidslinks.com/pcm/padres/

Index

About the Authors

Dr. Jack Stephen Williams has worked as an archaeologist and historian on various research projects in the United States, Mexico, South America, and Europe. Williams has a particular interest in the Native Americans and early colonization of the Southwest and California. He holds a doctoral degree in anthropology from the University of Arizona, and has written numerous books and articles. Williams lives in San Diego with his wife, Anita G. Cohen-Williams, and his daughter, Louise.

Thomas L. Davis, M.Div., M.A., was first introduced to the California Missions in 1957 by his grandmother. He began to collect books, photos, and other materials about the missions. He has, over the years, assembled a first-class research library about the missions and Spanish North America, and is a respected authority in his field. After ten years of working in the music business, Davis studied for the Catholic priesthood and was ordained for service in Los Angeles, California. Ten years as a Roman Catholic priest saw Father Thom make another life change. He studied at UCLA and California State University, Northridge, where he received his master of arts degree in history. He is a founding member of the California Mission Studies Association and teaches California and Latin American History at College of the Canyons, Santa Clarita, California. Davis lives in Palmdale, California, with his wife, Rebecca, and his son, Graham.